Helping Out

At the Aquarium

Judith Heneghan

WAYLAND

First published in 2011 by Wayland

Copyright © Wayland 2011

Wayland
Hachette Children's Books
338 Euston Road
London NW1 3BH

Wayland Australia
Level 17/207 Kent Street
Sydney, NSW 2000

Editor: Louise John
Designer: Robert Walster, Big Blu Design

British Library Cataloguing in Publication Data

Anderson, Judith, 1965-
  At the aquarium. -- (Helping out)
  1. Public aquariums--Juvenile literature. 2. Public
aquariums--Employees--Juvenile literature.
  I. Title II. Series
  597'.073-dc22

ISBN-13: 9780750264914

Printed in China
Wayland is a division of Hachette Children's Books, an
Hachette UK company.
www.hachette.co.uk

With thanks to The London Aquarium.

Picture acknowledgements
All photography by Andy Crawford other than:
The London Aquarium: pp6, 11, 13, 14, 19
Shutterstock: pp15 and 19
istock: pp7, 11 17 18 and 21

Disclaimer
The website addresses (URLs) included in this
book were valid at the time of going to press.
However, because of the nature of the Internet, it is
possible that some addresses may have changed,
or sites may have changed or closed down since
publication. While the author and Publisher regret
any inconvenience this may cause the readers, no
responsibility for any such changes can be accepted
by either the author or the Publisher.

Contents

Visiting the aquarium   4

Looking in the tanks   6

Food preparation   8

Feeding the rays   10

Water samples   12

The rainforest area   14

Feeding the sharks!   16

Coral reef zone   18

Feeding the turtles   20

Time to go home   22

Glossary   24

Index   24

Visiting the aquarium

Today, Lola and her mum are visiting the **aquarium**. Lola is going to help look after the fish and other sea creatures with Ash, one of the aquarists. An **aquarist** is someone who cares for animals in an aquarium.

Lola and her mum arrive at the aquarium.

Ash meets Lola and her mum at the entrance. She gives Lola a special shirt that all the aquarists wear and Lola goes downstairs to get changed.

Ash tells Lola what they'll be doing that day.

LOLA'S DIARY

Today is going to be a great day. Ash says I can help feed the turtles later on. I'm so excited!

Looking in the tanks

First, Ash shows Lola some of the **display tanks**. They see starfish, anemones, some herring and a blue lobster called Hamish. These animals live in cold seas like the Atlantic Ocean.

Blue lobsters are quite rare. They produce lots of protein, which gives them their blue colour.

That's AMAZING!

Scientists say that our oceans contain most of the world's animal species, including those that no one has discovered yet!

In the rock pool area people can touch starfish and shore crabs. The crabs and starfish only stay in the rock pool for two hours at a time. Then Ash moves them into a separate tank where they can recover from all the attention!

These anemones use their tentacles to catch tiny bits of food.

This shore crab moves very quickly.

Food preparation

Next Ash takes Lola to the food preparation area. Today she will help feed the rays, the sharks and the turtles. They eat fish such as sprats, whiting and squid, which are stored in a giant freezer.

Lola pulls on some gloves to keep her hands clean.

LOLA'S DIARY

The food preparation room stinks of fish! I didn't like it, but Ash says she's used to it. Getting the fish ready was the slimiest job ever!

The food isn't ready yet, though. Ash shows Lola how to put a **vitamin** tablet inside each piece of fish. Vitamins help keep the sharks and turtles healthy.

The vitamin tablets will be hidden inside the fish.

Lola puts a vitamin tablet inside this squid.

Feeding the rays

The rays are fed first. They live in a shallow tank, or **lagoon**, along with spider crabs and lesser-spotted dogfish. Ash shows Lola how to use a special rod to place pieces of fish on the bottom of the lagoon.

That's AMAZING!

There are around 600 types of ray. Some rays have stingers in their tails, but most can't sting.

The rays eat the pieces of fish from the bottom of the tank.

When the rays have eaten, Lola throws some cockles and sprats into the water for the crabs and the dogfish.

The rays have a wide, flat body with eyes on top and a mouth underneath.

Spider crabs got their name because they have long legs, just like a spider!

Water samples

After feeding the rays, Ash asks Lola to collect some water samples. The water must be tested every day to make sure it is clean and has the right amount of salt in it to keep the animals healthy.

Lola collects a water sample from the ray lagoon.

Lola and Ash collect water from the ray lagoon and from the octopus tank. They take the water samples to the lab, where they do a **dip test** with a little stick. Fortunately, the water is fine.

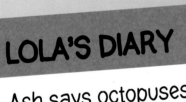

LOLA'S DIARY

Ash says octopuses are clever, curious and good at escaping! This one is called a Lesser Octopus. Its tentacles felt really sticky!

The dip stick changes colour when it touches the water sample.

The rainforest area

Lola visits the rainforest section next. Rainforests are found in hot, wet parts of the world. The fish and reptiles there live in warm freshwater rivers rather than cold salty seas.

Ed the catfish has long barbs, like whiskers. Barbs help catfish find food along the bottom of dark rivers.

Cuban crocodiles are now an endangered species.

Lola sees red-bellied piranha fish, a giraffe-nosed catfish called Ed, and two rare Cuban crocodiles called Sugar and Spice. Then she feeds the pufferfish. They eat fish flakes.

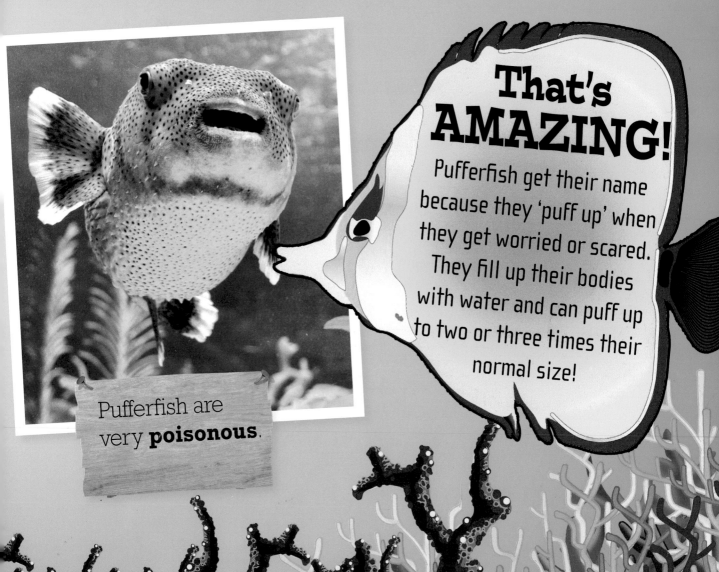

Pufferfish are very **poisonous**.

That's AMAZING!

Pufferfish get their name because they 'puff up' when they get worried or scared. They fill up their bodies with water and can puff up to two or three times their normal size!

Feeding the sharks!

After lunch it's time to feed the sharks! Ash takes Lola to the top of the huge shark tank. Then Lola puts on a safety jacket and some gloves. She can see the sharks swimming in the water below her.

Lola has fun throwing squid to the sharks!

Lola tempts Zippy with food on the end of a pole.

Lola takes a squid with a vitamin tablet inside it and throws it into the tank. The sharks are hungry, but two sand tiger sharks called Zippy and Bungle are fussy. They will only eat fish from the end of a pole.

LOLA'S DIARY

The sharks are fed three times a week. Ash says they eat between 20-25 kilos of fish each week. That's a lot of fish!

Coral reef zone

Lola visits the coral reef zone next, and must climb up a ladder to reach the top of the tanks. It's worth it though, because lots of little fish come rushing to the surface when they see Lola's bright blue shirt.

A coral reef provides excellent shelter for these fish.

That's AMAZING!

Coral is made up of thousands of tiny animals called **polyps**. When the polyps die, they form a hard reef.

Wanda the copper-banded butterflyfish is quite tame!

Wanda, a copper-banded butterflyfish, pokes her snout out of the water to take fish flakes from Lola's hand. But not all coral reef fish are safe. Some, like the stonefish, have a dangerous sting.

Stonefish look like part of the reef. Watch out though – they have poisonous spines along their backs!

Feeding the turtles

Lola has had an exciting day so far. It's not over yet, though. The green turtles are still waiting for their meal! Another aquarist, called Kim, shows her how to feed two sisters called White and Phoenix.

Kim and Lola use the feeding pole.

LOLA'S DIARY

Feeding the turtles was amazing! I could get really close to them and touch them. I got splashed a few times, too!

White and Phoenix are eight years old. In the wild, green turtles can live for up to 150 years if they manage to avoid **polluted** water and **hazards** like plastic bags. Turtles in the wild sometimes swallow plastic bags, mistaking them for jellyfish.

Lola has a turn at feeding Phoenix by herself.

Time to go home

When Lola and Ash have finished feeding the turtles, it's almost time to go home. Lola's mum has come to collect Lola, but Ash has one last surprise for her.

It's hard to leave the fish behind!

This tooth is from a brown shark. It's very sharp.

"This brown shark tooth is for you," she says. "Thank you for all your hard work today." "Thank you!" says Lola. "I've had the best day ever."

Lola and her mum say goodbye.

Glossary

Aquarist someone who cares for animals in an aquarium

Aquarium a place where fish and sea creatures are kept in tanks for visitors to see

Dip test a test where special sticks are dipped into the water to see how clean it is

Display tanks large tanks in the aquarium with glass fronts for visitors to look through

Hazards dangers in the environment

Lagoon a small body (or tank) of water that is joined to a larger one

Poisonous substances that can damage or harm the body

Polluted made unclean or dirty

Polyps a small growth that looks like a stalk

Vitamin substances that the body needs to keep it healthy

Index

anemones 7

aquarist 4, 5

butterflyfish 19

catfish 14, 15

coral reef 18, 19

crabs 7, 10, 11

crocodile 14, 15

dogfish 10, 11

food preparation 8

herring 6

lobster 6

octopus 13

piranhas 15

pufferfish 15

rays 8, 10, 11, 12, 13

sharks 8, 9, 16, 23

squid 9, 17

starfish 6, 7

stonefish 19

trout 22

turtles 5, 8, 9, 20, 21

vitamin 9, 17

Helping Out

Contents of titles in the series:

FARM

An early start
Cleaning the cow barn
Milking time
Feeding the calves
Cleaning the equipment
Feeding the cows
Chewing the cud
A visit from the vet
More milking
Time to go home

ZOO

Meeting the keepers
Looking around
Important jobs
Preparing the food
Meeting the lemurs
Feeding the lemurs
Cleaning and sweeping
Lemur play
Lemur babies
A brilliant day

AQUARIUM

Visiting the aquarium
Looking in the tanks
Food preparation
Feeding the rays
Water samples
The rainforest area
Feeding the sharks
Coral reef zone
Feeding the turtles
Time to go home

DOG RESCUE CENTRE

Saying hello
Meeting the dogs
A new arrival
Cleaning the kennels
Time for a walk
Feeding the puppies
A visit to the vet
Training fun
Finding a home
Time to say goodbye

WAYLAND